THE EDI[illegible]RSE FROM MASSACH[illegible]TS

A RECORD OF ONE YEAR'S PERSONAL SERVICE WITH THE BRITISH EXPEDITIONARY FORCE IN FRANCE

BOULOGNE — THE SOMME
1916-1917

With An Account Of
The Imprisonment, Trial, And Death
of Nurse Edith Cavell

First Published By W. A. Butterfield, Boston, M.A., 1917

British Library Cataloguing In Publication Data

A Record of This Publication is available from the British Library

ISBN 1846852021

978-1-84685-202-2

Published 2006 by
Diggory Press Ltd,
Three Rivers, Minions, Liskeard,
Cornwall, PL14 5LE, UK
WWW.DIGGORYPRESS.COM

Printed on acid free Paper

PART I

THE EDITH CAVELL NURSE FROM MASSACHUSETTS

THE WAR LETTERS OF ALICE FITZGERALD
Edited by Ella Lyman Cabot

Page 5

PART II

THE IMPRISONMENT, TRIAL, AND DEATH OF NURSE EDITH CAVELL

Page 51

PART I

THE EDITH CAVELL NURSE FROM MASSACHUSETTS

THE EDITH CAVELL NURSE FROM MASSACHUSETTS

INTRODUCTION

EDITH CAVELL'S story is of a singular beauty. With solicitude for her enemy's women, the German pupil-nurses in her training school at Brussels, she protected them from possible unkindness at the hands of the outraged Belgians, by herself taking them, at the beginning of the war, to the borders of their own land. And back at Brussels she nursed her enemy's wounded.

At her trial, she made no specious defence. With unclouded soul, she consented to her own death by giving the court the truth — that she had indeed helped her countrymen and the men of Belgium, her adopted home. For these friends she laid down her life. Is there greater love than this?

"After three weeks of solitary confinement, she said that she had found in prison kindness and peace of soul. For the enemy who first attempted to deceive our American representative, and then set aside his touching prayer, and that of the Spanish ambassador, for even a brief delay — for this enemy she had no condemnation. 'We must have,' she said, 'no hatred or bitterness.'

"As far as may be in her spirit, and believing that her execution struck at the heart of Christianity and of chivalry — we, American citizens, have asked the English director of military surgery to accept, for the rest of the war, the services of the Edith Cavell Memorial Nurse from Massachusetts. The offer, though unconditional, is made in the hope that it may be this nurse's high fortune to serve not only the Allies' heroic wounded but their prisoners."

The foregoing statement, published one year ago, had its origin in a memorial service, in honor of Edith Cavell, held in Steinert Hall, Boston, December 11, 1915. Professor George Herbert Palmer presided, and Mrs. Jessie D. Hodder, Fred B. Lund, M.D., and the

Rev. Samuel McChord Crothers spoke. It was then decided that an "Edith Cavell Nurse from Massachusetts" should be offered to the English Government to serve, with the British Expeditionary force in France, for the duration of the war.

The raising of the necessary funds and the far more difficult task of choosing a nurse whose spirit and capacity would fit her for her task, was entrusted to this committee. Money sufficient for salary and expenses for one year was promptly subscribed, and a nurse of exceptional attainments and personal distinction was discovered. Miss Alice L. F. Fitzgerald, the nurse in question, is fortunate in her previous experience. After graduating from the Johns Hopkins School, she superintended two training schools for nurses, became head of the operating room at the Bellevue Hospital, New York, and later worked with the Italian Red Cross for the Messina earthquake sufferers. For her devotion in that service she was decorated by the Italian Government.

Miss Fitzgerald's services in memory of Edith Cavell were accepted by the British Government. She has just completed her first year of work for the wounded, British, Colonial, and German, on the English front in France.

William Roscoe Thayer
Philip Cabot
Rosalind Huidekopeh Greene
Henry Copley Greene
William Ernest Hocking

Edith Cavell Committee

THE TREASURER'S REPORT
EDITH CAVELL FUND

January 17, 1916 to March 1, 1917		**DR**	**CR**
1916	Amount of Contributions		$2400.00
	Miss Alice L F Fitzgerald- Salary, 12 months	$600.00	
	Expenses: steamship fare, uniforms, kit, board and lodging for 12 months	$963.88	
May 8	12 dozen Rubber Gloves	$54.00	
	12 dozen thermometers	$72.00	
	Express charges	$10.65	
Oct 14	Gramophone & Records	$53.48	
Cash in hand March 1, 1917		$645.99	
TOTAL		**$2400.00**	**$2400.00**

The committee wishes to express its appreciation of the interest shown by the Dana Hall School of Wellesley, which released Miss Fitzgerald from work in the school, and paid for her passage to Europe.

The committee wishes also to acknowledge the generosity of Mr. A. H. Atkins, the Boston sculptor, who contributed his skill and talent in modelling the Edith Cavell medal which Miss Fitzgerald wears; and the kindness of the Gorham Manufacturing Co., which executed this medal in silver, free of charge.

Funds are needed to carry this work through its second year. When you have read the first year's work by the Edith Cavell Nurse from Massachusetts, we are confident that, if you are already a subscriber, you will renew your subscription, and that if not, you will wish to send in your first donation. All gifts, whether large or small, will be welcomed: they should be sent to

Philip Cabot, Treasurer,
111 Devonshire St., Boston, Mass.

PREFACE

THE spirit in which Miss Fitzgerald is carrying out her mission, and something of what that spirit means to her wounded in France, may be inferred from the following record. These brief extracts, from her letters to members of the Committee and to other friends in America and in France, tell us little of what she feels. Their unconsciousness makes them the more telling. It gives them, as we believe the reader will inevitably feel, a place heroic as it is humble, among the first-hand documents of the war.

THE EDITH CAVELL NURSE FROM MASSACHUSETTS

I

LONDON

FEB. 29 - MARCH 8, 1916.

I LANDED quite safely in Liverpool yesterday after a beautiful trip. I can hardly wait to get to work: the atmosphere is so tense, and no one is idling.

* * * * *

Yesterday I had a charming personal note from the Surgeon General, asking me to go and see him. Of course I went to the War Office at once. I had a delightful interview with Sir Alfred Keogh, who said he would send me to France as near the Front as a nurse can go! I then saw Miss Beecher, the Matron in Chief of the Nursing Service, who enrolled me with the rank of "Sister" and gave me directions for getting my equipment. I am now waiting for orders to leave, and hope to be off within a week. It seems too good to be true. Several people I have met, and Sir Alfred Keogh particularly, seemed to be very grateful to you all for sending over a nurse.

* * * * *

I hope that the Censor passed my cable telling you of my good fortune at receiving orders to leave for France at once. If my uniforms had been finished, I would have left today. One of the matrons on duty in France has been held back in order to escort me over, which is remarkably kind and thoughtful. My kit is ready, standing in the corner of the room, all packed in one large canvas bag: it contains the bed and mattress, pillow, sleeping bag, wash-stand, bath, chair, table, lantern, and many other necessities. Packing it is an art, I assure you. I hope that I can take it all back to America after the war, as it will make quite an interesting exhibit for your committee and contributors.

I shall not know where I am going until I reach France and find orders there.

II

BOULOGNE

MARCH 9 - MAY 9, 1916.

I MUST say again and again that I have found such endless kindness, consideration, and courtesy that it makes me feel very small and unworthy.

I crossed over to France last week, and after one day's rest was attached to a large military hospital at the Boulogne base. I have been so dead tired that I could hardly crawl when night came, with the rush and strangeness of it all. I shall probably stay here until I am a little familiar with the very intricate military routine and discipline and the very complicated record-keeping, etc. The nursing, with a few exceptions, is not so very different. I feel that I shall soon be helpful enough to do "my bit."

The English Tommies are the most wonderful men, — never a grumble, never a loud word, and they stand pain like super-human beings. It is best not to stop and think too much; one could never do the work.

I have been asked so often if more Edith Cavell nurses were coming. I wish some other States could follow your lead and send nurses; perhaps some could go to France, others to the English Red Cross, and to St. John's Ambulance, and so distribute them around.

* * * * *

I received yesterday, by registered package, the medal. I cannot tell you, how proud I am to have it, nor how beautiful I think it is. Can you tell Mr. Atkins for me that it has been so much admired by many whose opinion is worth while? As a design of a nurse it is by far the most beautiful I have seen.

We are busy: convoys nearly every night. Acting as an assistant to the head of a ward, I have an opportunity to see the administration side and to help with the actual work.

Please tell Francesca that I have decided to spend her 60 cents in buying a plant for the ward, as the poor fellows love the green, and the plant will last a long time.

* * * * *

It is still bitterly cold, and it was snowing two days ago. I am rather glad that I am now quartered in a comfortable hotel instead of a tent!

I wish I could convey to you the appreciation of those in authority for the gift of a nurse which you have made to them. Only yesterday Sir Arthur Sloggett, the Director General of all the British hospitals in France, called on me and told me how welcome I was and how glad they are to have me. They gave me two stripes, the highest any reserve Sister ever gets, and a ward of 22 beds within the first few weeks. I feel they have been very kind and confident!

The weather is getting warm at last and it is very nice to see the sun shine again. We are being visited by an enemy aeroplane every now and then. Of course we do exactly what we should not do; we rush out and watch the anti air-craft guns shelling it, and so run the double risk of being hit by a bomb or by the returning shells. It is too tempting, and so exciting, to see the shells get so near it, and yet miss it.

One thing has struck me forcibly lately, — the one thing our country has overlooked in its many helpful activities, — and that is recreation for the wounded. You should see the pleasure that an occasional band concert or a theatrical performance gives to these poor fellows. While listening to one of the crack English bands the other day, which goes from hospital base to hospital base, I was thinking how fine it would be if Sousa or someone equally good could be induced to come over and help to give the poor fellows a treat. We nurse them, and feed them; and it would be nice to give them a little pleasure besides. I am sure that you will see how much a little recreation means to a man straight from the trenches. Miss Lena Ashwell, the English actress, sends out members of her company and other artists once each month; they go from hospital to hospital, and give the very best of programs.

What a surprise to all when the Russians landed in Marseilles!

III

SOMEWHERE IN FRANCE, MAY 9 - SEPT. 15, 1916.

I HAD my orders on Monday; and on Tuesday came to "Somewhere in France," only a few kilometres from the firing line, and in the midst of intense activity. Such endless processions of transports, men, supplies, ammunition, despatch bearers. . . .The noise of shelling is quite plain; and sometimes the bursting shells can be seen at night. The papers say that the Germans are going to make their next effort against our lines up here; but we are ready for them.

* * * * *

On my arrival, at about 8 p.m., I was shown to my tent, and I had my first chance to unpack and use my precious kitbag. I was surprised at the ease with which I put up a bed, a wash-stand, a table, and chair in a short time. These pieces are so wonderfully well made, and the parts fit in so beautifully, that any one can put them up. Wonderful how comfortable it all was!

Now I am in a hut, but still use all my own kit things. I am in a new hospital which only opened ten days ago, and we expect to be very busy some day. Aeroplanes, captive balloons, despatch bearers, motor transports, etc. are continually us that blood is being shed not so very far away.

There are many Australian nurses with us here, but the Canadian nurses are mostly kept with their own units. I saw the Harvard unit hospital one day. They are very highly thought of, and are doing good work. I am certainly putting "Massachusetts on the map," for so many people want to know where I come from and why I am here.

* * * * *

My patients have been enjoying a gramophone sent by the Red Cross for the use of the wards; they are like children over it! You can imagine these poor men, fresh from trench life and the sight of all horrors, but now lying in nice white beds and listening to familiar tunes. Giving them such pleasures is part of the game, and not the least by any means, I assure you.

The Colonials, Australians, New Zealanders, Canadians, Indians, are splendid men, and eager for a hot fight. They will get their wish I fancy. I am writing this in the ward facing a row of fine, brave fellows who have been fighting for their country and the just cause. They lie here without a grumble or complaint, just waiting to be sent back to it if they are well enough to go; and "going back" is much harder in my opinion than going for the first time.

The gloves and thermometers will come in most usefully, also the cases which have been sent to me from the Peter Bent Brigham Committee.

* * * * *

Yes indeed, I can use writing paper, plain chocolate, and any games. I believe that I should have greatly increased in value, had I been given a gramophone to bring with me. One Sister has such a nice one, fitting into a travelling case. If you know any one keen to give one away, do think of me. It does one's heart good to see the poor fellows cheer up over a good record. One of their favorites is "Take me back to U. S. A." Very catchy, and I like it too!

We have two German prisoners wounded, but not in my ward.

* * * * *

You will be interested to know that I was the only person in the hospital who could talk to our wounded prisoners. They were here for two days; I felt very deeply the strength of my mission, when I was working and interpreting for them.

Yesterday we had some distinguished visitors, among them Dr. A. Carrel of the Rockefeller in New York. He has worked with so many Hopkins people that we had much to chatter about. Sir Arthur Sloggett, the Director General of the Medical Service in France, or D. G. for short, I have met twice. He is very charming. In fact the "Edith Cavell Nurse from Massachusetts" has many distinguished and interested visitors; and many nice things are said about Massachusetts.

We have very busy days followed by very quiet ones waiting for the next convoy after a night of fighting. We are really a clearing house to relieve congestion nearer the front, and do not keep the patients very long. Apart from the hospital work, life is very interesting. You walk down to the village, and meet column after column of large motor lorries carrying ammunition or supplies, large cannon being pulled by the most powerful motor engines, detachments of cavalry, bicycle corps. . . . War is such a business now! So much system, so much planning!

We have spread out into a large number of tents, ready to cover 1000 wounded. The enemy has been flying over us very frequently with more or less success. But we are very carefully guarded by aeroplanes scouting whenever weather permits.

* * * * *

A most beautiful air fight took place over us this a.m.: eleven machines all maneuvering and shooting. Ours routed the enemy before he had done anything, to us at least. One stood there watching, quite forgetful that something might fall on one at any time, even if only an empty shell!

I have a gas mask at hand for emergency use and wear my identification disk around my neck, so am taking all precautions.

Ten boxes have come from Boston and are most welcome, sent by the Peter Bent Brigham Committee. I shall be more than delighted to get the gramophone[1], chocolates, etc. I know they will give much pleasure to these brave fellows.

* * * * *

I believe that we are starting at last, and that "something will be doing" from now on. The air is filled with tenseness and expectation, and incidentally with aeroplane scouts. We were bombed the other day: that is, the village a few hundred yards away. Many casualties and deaths. It may be our turn next. The Taubes came back the next day, but our scouts were after them.

It seems such a long time ago that I lived in a peaceful, noiseless atmosphere, that I wonder if such a thing still exists. As I write, the shelling along the front is something fearful in its angry, determined sounds! The sky is alive with aeroplanes of all kinds, the scouts, the battle planes. . . Some fly so low that they almost touch the poles of our tents.

---

1 Sent by the Edith Cavell Committee.

My cousin in Baltimore sent some cigarettes and some chocolate for the soldiers, which came through without trouble or delay, and were so much enjoyed. If you hear of any one wanting to do likewise, please encourage them. The fact that these things had come from so far seemed to add to their value. They were sent c/o the War Office, London.

I have a very tender spot in my heart for the "Colonials," Australians, Canadians, New Zealanders, etc. I know them the moment they open their mouths; and they know I am a sort of "Colonial" myself, the moment I speak; and we soon understand each other beautifully. Their views are very different from the views of the pure Englishman. It is interesting to study the changes. They are so absolutely reckless and frank! There is rarely a "hot place" on the front where they will not be found. This very moment some of them are doing a big piece of work.

The thermometer and gloves arrived quite safely and in good condition, two days ago[2]. I

[2] Sent by the Edith Cavell Committee.

wish that I might thank those who made it possible to send me these things. Rubber gloves are so necessary; for the wounds are all so badly infected that one's hands become a source of danger to others as well as to one's self. Within a few days, and in spite of all precautions, two of our surgeons have become infected from the wounds. One has been invalided home after facing the possible loss of his arm; the other is recovering here. You see practically every bullet or piece of shrapnel or other foreign body carries in pieces of dirty clothing, earth, etc.; and conditions are terrible.

We are not as busy at present as we were a few days ago, but these days of rest make it possible for us to keep up with the days of rush.

You would be surprised to see how very useful my languages are. Every German wounded prisoner we get, I have to interview and obtain particulars, besides censoring all their correspondence. It is the same with the French. As very few of the English Sisters have taken advantage of their stay in France to study the language, I am called upon to interpret upon all occasions.

Do you realize that I am on my sixth month? It does not seem possible that I left the U.S. A. so long ago.

* * * * *

I received yesterday a nice box containing two fine sets of checkers and boards, chocolates, much letter paper with envelopes and pencils, and playing cards. For all of these very many thanks to you and others responsible for the gifts.

Very busy at present with shifting forces. Our army corps is not actually the active one; but we await our turn patiently.

Dear Francesca: Your mother wrote and told me that you had saved $1 for me to spend on something for our wounded, and today I had the opportunity to do so. I have an old man in my ward who is 53, but in order to get into the army he "lied " and said he was 38! Do you think that was very wicked, or very brave? Well, he broke his pipe and lost his eyeglass-case in the trenches. So I bought him a pipe and a case for his eyeglasses. He was so pleased to know that it came from a little girl in America that he wrote the enclosed letter and asked me to send it to you. He is such a fine old man!

To the little girl who sent the present —

Dear little girl, it is more than kind of you so far away to think of the British soldiers in France. I am more than thankful to receive such a gift from you.

I am an old man, and have had little girls of my own, but they are all married. I have got two boys left, one 16 years and one 11 years of age. I have been out here as a volunteer for 6 months and I have been in the front lines; but I am sorry to say I am sent down as unfit. I may tell you, all the regiments that I have seen, the officers and men are all cheerful. I have been very well dealt with in this Hospital. The Sisters are very kind, especially Sister Fitzgerald. So, my little heroine, once more receive my very grateful thanks from

Your old soldier,
Pte James Wilson.

I have quite made up my mind that certainly there will be one more winter campaign at least, if not more! I have sent my passport to the Embassy in Paris for renewal. Weather delightful, cool and sunny, just right for fighting.

* * * * *

Will you tell Faith that I have been buying pipes and giving them in her name, as so many of the Tommies needed them? The nice old man who got Francesca's pipe reached home safely, and wrote me such a grateful little note!

We had a visit from the King and the Prince of Wales and suite lately, which pleased the patients immensely. The King looks well, but aged. I have come to the conclusion that even in the very small part that I play, each day makes me a week older. I cannot quite explain it. It is not only the hard work, but the whole situation and atmosphere in which we live. At night the firing line is all lighted by the star shells sent up to help locate positions. On a clear day, we can see much of the activities on the firing line: observation balloons, aeroplanes, shells bursting . . . It makes it all very vividly real that men are killing each other not so far away.

Most of the women around here are refugees from the invaded area, poor things. They live anywhere, anyhow, and just subsist on as little as possible. Their husbands, fathers, brothers are either fighting or dead. What have they to look forward to, with everything lost and their villages probably destroyed?

IV

AT A CASUALTY CLEARING STATION, SEPT. 16 - DEC. 31.

I AM on my way to 2/2 London Casualty Clearing Station, which will be my address for the present. I am very glad to be going where I am going; I fancy it will be hard work ahead.

* * * * *

I am in the thick of it, as this is the nearest Clearing Station to the Front. I assure you I am all but in the trenches! We are situated in a horseshoe, with the firing line on three sides. We can only walk a short distance in all directions for fear of getting shelled. Our quarters (nurses') are in small Bell Tents. I have a nice little one all to myself. Two days of pouring rain have made everything disappear under inches of dirty clay mud.

My costume these days consists of rubber, knee-deep boots, rubber coat, a sou'wester. Going in and out of tents, and even in the tents, which leak, nothing else is possible.

The shelling is continuous, air fights going on. We are advancing splendidly. German prisoners tell me they are very tired of the war, and have had so little to eat! I think the end is in sight.

* * * * *

We are on ground formerly occupied by Germans, and see the trenches, the empty shell cases, of the old scene of fighting. When I first came, there were no floors to the tents, only the bare ground. It rained for three days; and I got out of bed into a puddle every morning. The mud was something awful.

The work is of course of a most active sort. We get the patients by ambulances from the field hospitals, and we sort them. The operative cases are operated upon; those too ill to travel are settled comfortably; and others are dressed, fed, and sent on by train to the base. They pass through our hands by the hundreds. I could not imagine that men could live with such awful wounds; in civil life they would die of fright alone.

I am right in the thick of it now; and the shells whiz by our ears in great style. It is queer that, where there is such real danger, one does not think of it.

I have charge of two tents which hold from 60 to 70 wounded each, and they have been so covered with stretchers that I had to crawl in and out to get through. It is awfully hard work nursing a patient on a stretcher which only stands about 6" from the ground; and I sometimes wish I were not so tall!

We are in the wilderness; even newspapers do not come regularly; and as for mail, I have not seen any since I came. I was able to get money on my letter of credit at Abbeville where I stopped over, so I am settled for three or four months. Dr. Lord's little daughter sent me a second bundle of knitted wash rags, which were most welcome.

I am just as happy as the day is long, working in my little tent-ward, and trying to help the poor fellows. Soldiers are really wonderful. They go to fight with a smile; they come back half dead with a smile. The least we can do is to make them as happy and comfortable as we can. Nothing is too good for them.

I went through the wonderfully interesting spot quite lately, German dugouts, shell holes, craters, etc., etc. As far as noises are concerned, I do not believe there are any which I have not heard. If noises could kill, we should all be corpses. It is roar, roar, roar, day and night, — guns nearer by with their louder reports, air craft fights, anti-air-craft guns, bombs exploding, German shells whizzing over our camp. And with it all, it is a blessing to be busy.

As to the question of "leave," my getting away just now is absolutely impossible, unless I am taken in a "box" — which is perfectly possible. We are in constant danger from enemy shells; and the Taubes have dropped bombs only a few yards away from us.

About a week ago, in the middle of the night, I woke up at the sound of the dropping of bombs nearer and nearer, until one came down so near that the vibration simply knocked me out of bed. Such a noise! The shrapnel from it went through the roof of our two wards which were empty just then. If you go out walking, you are suddenly startled by the whizzing of a shell until you get quite jerky! I do not mind it a bit, however, and feel that there is great need of nurses 'way up front like this.

I suppose you have read about the "Tanks"? I went into one the other day, — pure cheek! Every one laughs, and says, "Trust U. S. A. to get there!" The officer in charge looked so surprised to see me, and said, "Where on earth did you drop from?"

Could I trouble you to have one thing sent out to me of which I am in urgent need? Refills for my flash-lamp, as we cannot get candles for love or money, and I must have some lighting.

* * * * *

The winter is with us. I am glad to say that huts have been put up for us. We left our tents ten days ago. The huts have roofs and sides of corrugated iron which will prevent shrapnel and small pieces of shell from reaching us. The tents were anything but safe.

I am crippled with chilblains on my feet and hands. Those on my feet are made worse by having to wear high rubber boots in this perpetual rain and mud. Never knew I had feet before.

* * * * *

Have I ever told you that my messing expenses here are just as they were before, that is, 4 francs daily? This month there will be some winter equipment, including a pair of rubber boots. Would you believe it possible that I have worn one pair down, in these few weeks, on account of the awful mud which they have sprinkled with the sharpest stones you ever saw, to prevent our sinking right in? Wandering around after dark, even with a hurricane lamp, is a dangerous performance.

I do hope that U. S. A. are going to take a stand about the submarines.

* * * * *

It is quite wonderful how these huts deaden the ceaseless noise of the shelling. At times I almost forget where I am, until "Big Liz" or some one else peals forth an extra loud salute. That "shakes" me back to the reality of the situation. I know you will all have a happy Xmas. I hear rumors of a turkey and plum pudding for our mess. It will taste very good after months of "bully beef" and tinned things. However, in spite of food and other things which are not quite perfect, I am feeling splendidly and not planning as yet on leave. I think I shall ask for it, however, before my 12 months are up, or I shall lose it altogether for this year.

V

LONDON AND BOULOGNE
JAN.-FEB., 1917.

I HAVE been granted 3 weeks' leave and shall report back for duty January the 22nd. I have no idea where I shall be sent on my return to France. I shall find my orders on landing.

The crossing is made quite horribly uncomfortable by having to wear a life belt. I can recommend it as an instrument of torture when you would like to lie back comfortably in a steamer chair!

* * * * *

After three weeks in London I came over on the 24th, and was delighted to find that my orders were to report at 13 General Hospital, where I started last March and where I was keenly anxious to return.

We live in billets here in a hotel, and the expenses will be higher than when we mess in camp.

It is awfully cold, in fact the coldest weather which has been known in years. As there is no heat in the building, I am still hugging my little oil lamp. But it is far more comfortable than a hut anyway!

*****

What an excitement over U. S. A. affairs! I am being greeted as a "half ally" now, waiting for the declaration of war to become a "full one." Things are getting very tense. The air is full of electricity or rather of activity: what? when? where?

Who knows?

PART II

EDITH CAVELL
HER IMPRISONMENT, TRIAL AND DEATH

THE MESSAGE OF EDITH CAVELL

A MEETING in honor of Edith Cavell was held at Steinert Hall on December 11. "In honor?" questioned Professor George H. Palmer, who presided. "It is difficult to find a suitable word to express our feeling. We cannot honor her. She gives us honor. But in this meeting tonight, held simultaneously with one in Canada, there is thanksgiving for her going up from two great countries at once."

In the courageous, self-forgetful, truth-loving life of Edith Cavell we meet, with an extraordinary sense of intimacy, a woman so beautiful of soul that I want every teacher in the land and every child in school to hear the story of her sacrifice.

Nine years ago she went to Brussels, and established a training school. Up to the time the war broke out hundreds of Belgian and German nurses had come to it. It was characteristic of Miss Cavell that fearing the indignation of the Belgians might make it difficult for the German nurses to get home, she herself escorted them safely across the frontier.

Then came the care of the wounded. She nursed Germans and Belgians alike during the long breathless year from August, 1914, to August, 1915. Suddenly she was arrested; held for ten weeks in prison; then summarily shot.

And why did Miss Cavell receive a sentence of death after a trial of two days? She had harbored and helped across the frontier some English and French soldiers and some young Belgians. When asked why she did this, she said that she thought that had she not done so they would have been shot by the Germans, and that she only did her duty to her country in saving their lives. "Treason," the German military penal code called this act. Long ago in New England, Ralph Waldo Emerson wrote that no house was complete that did not have a room in which to hide a fugitive slave. Treason, did we call it?

At five in the afternoon of October 12 Edith Cavell was condemned to death. Next morning at 2 o'clock, the darkest hour of night, with no dawn lighting the sky, she was shot. Late the evening before an English chaplain, Mr. Gahan, was admitted to her cell to give her the Holy Communion. The words of that interview are precious, shining, miraculous. She said, smiling: "I am not afraid to die, I have seen death so often that it is not terrible to me." Then of her imprisonment, "I am so thankful for these ten weeks of quiet. Life has always been so hurried. They have been very good to me." And finally, "But I realize that patriotism is not enough; one must have no hatred, no bitterness." With her friend she recited the words of "Abide with Me," and when he said a last farewell, answered clear-eyed: "We shall meet again."

Gathered together at the memorial service for Miss Cavell we found, I think, pearls of great price. The qualities of courage and of truth have often been thought of as belonging to men rather than to women. Miss Cavell had courage to face both life and death. In loyalty to truth she calmly gave evidence that made her condemnation certain. That death she met for her country and even more for God. Her last words fall like words from the Gospel: "One must have no hatred or bitterness." Neutrality is a colorless and often a craven attitude; forgiveness of enemies is the dawn of a renewed Christianity. "If thine enemy hunger, feed him." She had fed the wounded German soldiers. "Bless them that curse you." "They have been very good to me," she said. "I am thankful for the peace of these ten weeks." Surely to find peace through days when one's life is at stake passeth understanding, and brings the spirit of heaven upon earth.

At the memorial meeting of which I spoke, it was voted that a fund be raised in honor of Miss Cavell to offer the British War Office a nurse who should serve at the front, nursing both the English and their wounded prisoners. This use of her fund would, I think, satisfy Miss Cavell. "Her execution," said Samuel M. Crothers, "is a deed that strikes at the heart of Christianity and of chivalry." True, and for that reason, only the spirit of Christianity itself and of womanhood, such as that of Edith Cavell, are strong enough to rise unharmed from the agony of this war, irresistible, forever returning blessings for curses.

Ella Lyman Cabot.

I
EDITH CAVELL [3]

EDITH CAVELL was born in 1872 at the village of Swardeston, Norfolk, of which her father was rector. During her childhood, Florence Nightingale's life-work was beginning to bear fruit in a great development of trained nursing in England. The girls of Edith Cavell's generation found a wonderful field of service opening before them. Edith Cavell herself was one of those that entered it.

Miss Cavell began her training at the London Hospital when she was twenty-one. She qualified

[3] Reprinted, in abridged form, from "The Death of Edith Cavell," a pamphlet published by the Daily News and Ledger, London and Manchester.

in 1896, and distinguished herself by ten years of responsible work in England. In 1906 Miss Cavell was asked to be the first directress of a "Belgian School of Certified Nurses" in process of foundation at Brussels. In addition to her professional experience and enthusiasm, she was especially qualified for the task by the fact that she had spent several years of her girlhood in Brussels at school, and so was already familiar with Belgian life. The patrons of the new Nursing Institute looked forward to the great development of the nursing profession in Belgium under Miss Cavell. But in the eighth year of her pioneer-work came the war.

II
THE ARREST

SHE was spending a holiday with her mother in England at the moment war broke out. There would be work in Brussels for her to do, and she returned immediately to do it.

She arrived in time to share the terrible experience of the German entry into the Belgian capital. The Training Institute transformed itself under Miss Cavell's direction into a hospital for sick and wounded soldiers. Belgians, Frenchmen, and Englishmen, as well as the German invaders, all came under her impartial care. She nursed friend and foe with single-minded devotion. But she did not limit her services to this. She took counsel with her

Belgian friends, and succeeded, with their assistance, in conveying many of her French, British, and Belgian patients, as they recovered, to the farther side of the Dutch Frontier, that they might fight again for the common cause instead of undergoing whatever fate the German authorities allotted to convalescent prisoners-of-war. She also helped in the escape of Belgian civilians of military age, who had been overtaken, before they could join the colors, by the rapidity of the German advance, and were being held at home in virtual captivity.

So she worked for a year — a year of military nursing, and nine months of friendship in need to her friends and fellow-countrymen — until the German Administration in Belgium discovered her share in the escapes.

On August 5th, 1915, Edith Cavell was arrested at her hospital by soldiers, and carried away to the military prison of St.-Gilles.

III
THE AMERICAN LEGATION INTERVENES

EDITH CAVELL had been three weeks in prison before her family in England heard of her arrest, and then they only heard of it privately from a traveller who happened to have come from Belgium since the event. They communicated the news to the Foreign Office, and action was immediately taken by Sir Edward Grey.

Sir Edward sent a note on August 26th to Mr. Page, the United States Ambassador in London, requesting him to inquire of the United States Minister at Brussels by telegraph, whether the report of Miss Cavell's arrest were correct, and, if it were, what reason had been alleged in explanation.

Mr. Page telegraphed to his colleague at Brussels, Mr. Whitlock, next morning; and four days later, on August 31st, Mr. Whitlock addressed an inquiry on the subject to Baron von der Lancken, the chief of the "Political Department" (Politische Abteilung) of the German Military Government in the conquered territory. After waiting ten days without being vouchsafed an answer, Mr. Whitlock followed it up in another note on September 10th:

> The United States Minister presents his compliments to Baron von der Lancken and has the honour to draw his Excellency's attention to his letter of the 31st August, respecting the arrest of Miss Cavell, to which no reply has yet been received.
>
> As the Minister has been requested by telegraph to take charge of Miss Cavell's defence without delay, he would be greatly obliged if Baron von der Lancken would enable him to take forthwith such steps as may be necessary for this

defence, and to answer by telegraph to the despatch which he has received.

The Chief of the German "Political Department" could not ignore the American Minister at Brussels a second time. Baron von der Lancken wrote in reply:

POLITICAL DEPARTMENT
OF THE GOVERNOR-GENERAL IN BELGIUM.
I. 6940.

BRUSSELS,
September 12, 1915.

In reply to your Excellency's note of the 31st ultimo, I have the honour to inform you that Miss Edith Cavell was arrested on the 5th August, and that she is at present in the Military prison of St.-Gilles.

She has herself admitted that she concealed in her house French and English soldiers, as well as Belgians of military age, all desirous of proceeding to the front. She has also admitted having furnished these soldiers with the money necessary for their journey to France, and having facilitated their departure from Belgium by providing them with guides, who enabled them to cross the Dutch Frontier secretly.

Miss Cavell's defence is in the hands of the advocate Braun, who, I may add, is already in touch with the competent German authorities.

In view of the fact that the Department of the Governor-General as a matter of principle does not allow accused persons to have any interviews whatever, I much regret my inability to procure for M. de Leval permission to visit Miss Cavell as long as she is in solitary confinement.

I avail, etc.,
LANCKEN

IV
M. DE LEVAL TAKES STEPS

M. DE LEVAL, whose name is referred to in Baron von der Lancken's final reply, is a Belgian advocate retained as Legal Counsellor by the United States Legation in the Belgian capital. In a report which he drew up for Mr. Whitlock after the tragedy was over, he very clearly describes the successive steps he took in the case.

As he might not see Miss Cavell, M. de Leval got into touch with her advocate, M. Braun. At his request M. Braun came to call on him at the Legation a few days later. It appeared that he was a member of the Brussels Bar, and that he had been asked by personal friends of Miss

Cavell to defend her before the German Court; "but owing (he said) to some unforeseen circumstances he was prevented from pleading before that Court." This, then, was the outcome of his dealings with "the competent German authorities." M. Braun added that "he had asked M. Kirschen, a member (likewise) of the Brussels Bar, and his friend, to take up the case and plead for Miss Cavell, and that M. Kirschen had agreed to do so."

V
THE ADVOCATE KIRSCHEN

M. DE LEVAL took the only possible course. He put himself in touch with M. Kirschen, who, after a slight further delay, accorded him the interview for which he asked. In the course of this interview M. Kirschen

(i) Informed him that the lawyers defending prisoners before the German Military Court were not allowed to see their clients before the trial, and were not shown any document of the prosecution. This, he added, was in accordance with the German military rules.

(ii) He declared that the hearing of the trial of such cases was carried out very carefully, and that, in his opinion, although it was not possible to see the client before the trial, in fact the trial itself developed so carefully and so slowly, that it was generally possible to have a fair knowledge of all the facts and to present a good defence for the prisoner. This would specially be the case for Miss Cavell, because the trial would be rather long, as she was prosecuted with thirty-four other prisoners.

(iii) On learning of M. de Leval's intention to be present at the trial, so as to watch the case, M. Kirschen strongly dissuaded him from doing so. He thought that if the Germans would admit M. de Leval's presence, which was very doubtful, it would in any case cause prejudice to Miss Cavell.

(iv) He promised that he would keep M. de Leval posted on all the developments which the case might take, and would report to him the exact charges that were brought against Miss Cavell, and the facts concerning her that would be disclosed at the trial, so as to allow him to judge for himself about the merits of the case.

(v) He insisted that he would do all that was humanly possible to defend Miss Cavell to the best of his ability.

With this, M. Kirschen took his departure, leaving things very much where they were before.

So darkness descended again on the case for another three weeks, until, on Monday, October 4th, M. Kirschen duly notified M. de Leval that the trial was to begin on the following Thursday, October 7th.

Upon the receipt of this news, M. de Leval immediately wrote M. Kirschen a letter "confirming in writing in the name of the Legation the arrangement that had been made between them at their previous interview."

Brussels,
October 5, 1915.

Sir,

I thank you for the letter you were so good as to address to M. de Leval, in which you informed him that Miss Caveil's case would come before the court-martial at 8 a.m. next Thursday. In pursuance of the arrangement already come to, I should be most grateful if you will be so good as to send me, after the hearing, a memorandum setting forth the acts for which Miss Cavell is being prosecuted, and stating the charges which are brought against her at the hearing, and also the sentence passed.

I am, etc.
(For the Minister),
G. de Leval,
Legal Adviser to the Legation.

This letter was delivered to M. Kirschen by a messenger of the Legation, and M. de Leval waited anxiously for his next report.

VI
THE TRIAL

ON Thursday, October 7th, the trial of Edith Cavell and her fellow-prisoners began. It was nine weeks since her first arrest and imprisonment. That had been on August 5th, and all this time she had been retained (unconvicted though she was) in solitary confinement, cut off from communion with her friends and from all intercourse whatsoever with the outside world.

M. de Leval has embodied in his report a very exact account of the proceedings, which he afterwards obtained from some one who had taken part in them. We may say at once that this informant was not M. Kirschen.

"Miss Cavell (says M. de Leval's informant) was prosecuted for having helped English and

French soldiers, as well as Belgian young men, to cross the frontier and to go over to England. She had admitted by signing a statement before the day of the trial, and by public acknowledgment in Court, in the presence of all the other prisoners, and the lawyers, that she was guilty of the charges brought against her."

The German Military Code says:

"Will be sentenced to death for treason any person who is guilty of ... conducting soldiers to the enemy . . . (viz.: 'dem Feinde Mannschaften zufuhrt')-

"The penalties apply, in case of war, to foreigners as well as to Germans."

Now Edith Cavell did not succor her friends and compatriots in distress because she thought she could do so with impunity. She succored them, in the first place, from pure humanity — a humanity which has been shown by women through all ages to fugitives wounded and in distress; and, in the second place, because she thought (as she declared in Court) that she was doing her unquestionable duty to her country. But she knew all the while that she was doing it at the risk of her life; and she willingly responded to her inquisitors by an admission of all, and more than all, their charges.

In defending their conduct, the Germans lay great stress on the fact that their victim had done what she did with open eyes. Here, for instance, is a quotation from a statement to an American journalist by Herr Zimmermann, the Imperial German Under-Secretary-of-State for Foreign Affairs:

"In the Cavell case we are in presence of a well-thought-out, *world-wide* conspiracy which succeeded for nine months in rendering the most valuable service to the enemy to the disadvantage of our Army.

"Countless British, Belgian, and French soldiers are now again fighting in the Allies' ranks who owe their escape from Belgium to the activity of the band now sentenced, at the head of which stood Miss Cavell.

"With such a situation under the eyes of the authorities only the utmost severity can bring relief, and a Government violates the most elementary duty towards its army that does not adopt the strictest measures."

Who were the Englishmen, Frenchmen, and Belgians in this case? They were not invaders, or raiders, or spies. They were men wounded or missing from armies fighting for the liberty of the country in which they found themselves, or they were citizens of that country seeking an opportunity to give her their service.

Most of them were natives and citizens of Belgium, while Edith Cavell — the "head of the conspiracy," as Herr Zimmermann prefers to call her — had come to Belgium, on the invitation of the Belgians themselves, to carry out a work of public beneficence, on which she had already been engaged for more than eight years. And the acts for which they were now arraigned were likewise acts of mercy, which women, at any rate (and many of the "band" were women, besides their "head"), have never refused to perform on behalf of fellow-creatures in distress.

These were the people against whom the German administration was obliged to "adopt the strictest measures," for fear of "violating the most elementary duty towards its army." Herr Zimmermann's phrases are so complacent and so officially correct, that it needs an effort to remind ourselves what that army actually was. It was the German Army which had invaded without provocation a country whose inviolability the German Government had solemnly guaranteed. It was the army which had treated the helpless and innocent population among whom it came as no invaded people for centuries had been treated by European soldiers — the army that plundered and burnt and slaughtered and ravished. The German Army, it is to be supposed, had committed itself to its career of "frightfulness" in Belgium in order not to fail in its duty towards the German Government; and now the Government was inflicting the same "frightfulness" on Miss Cavell in order to carry out its duty to the Army.

It is not an unimportant point that, even under the German Military Law by which she was tried, Edith Cavell was rendered amenable to the death-penalty only by evidence which she volunteered of her own accord, and which no one else could have obtained against her. M. de Leval's informant told him that:

"She had acknowledged not only that she had helped these soldiers to cross the frontier, but also that some of them had thanked her in writing when arriving in England. This last admission made her case so much the more serious, because if it only had been proved against her that she had helped the soldiers to traverse the Dutch Frontier, and no proof was produced that these soldiers had reached a country at war with Germany, she could only have been sentenced for an attempt to commit the 'crime,' and not for the 'crime' being duly accomplished."

That was one point in the case, but there is another which would have appealed still more directly to any judge. Edith Cavell was a nurse, constant to the ideals of her calling. If part of her efforts had been given, during those nine months, to assisting her convalescent patients to escape, her daily labors were spent, as they always had been, on the unconditional service of the sick. She had not only succored the English, French, and Belgian wounded that came under her care; she had nursed Germans as well — nursed them back to life that they might fight again for their own country, with just the same devotion as she displayed to those others whom she was sending home to fight for a cause which was hers as well as theirs.

That service to their wounded comrades should have made Edith Cavell's life sacred in the eyes of the German officers who condemned her to death. It should have reprieved her even if she had been a spy.

But the German authorities were not governed by such considerations.

"Once for all" (states Herr Zimmermann), "the activity of our enemies has been stopped, and the sentence has been carried out to *frighten* those who may presume on their sex to take part in enterprises punishable with death."

The narrative of the trial which M. de Leval had from his informant, and which he incorporated in his own Report, continues thus: "In her oral statement before the Court, Miss Cavell disclosed almost all the facts of the whole prosecution. She was questioned in German, an interpreter translating all the questions in French, with which language Miss Cavell was well acquainted. She spoke without trembling and showed a clear mind. Often she added some greater precision to her previous depositions.

"When she was asked why she helped these soldiers to go to England, she replied that she thought that if she had not done so they would have been shot by the Germans, and that therefore she thought she only did her duty to her country in saving their lives.

"*The Military Prosecutor, however, asked the Court to pass a death sentence on Miss Cavell* and eight other prisoners amongst the thirty-five. The Court did not seem to agree, and the judgment was postponed. The person informing me said he thought that the Court would not go to the extreme limit."

VII
KIRSCHEN'S SILENCE AND CONRAD'S ASSURANCES

THE Court rose on Friday, October 8th, one day after its sitting had begun. Meanwhile, M. de Leval was waiting for M. Kirschen's next communication. He did not expect to hear that the Court had risen — M. Kirschen had himself assured him that "the hearing would be carried out very carefully and the trial would be rather long." His astonishment was therefore considerable when he was informed by an outsider that "the trial had taken place, though no judgment would be reached till a few days later." This was on Saturday, October 9th, and not a word from M. Kirschen had been received.

"Receiving no report from M. Kirschen," continues M. de Leval, "I tried to find him, but failed. I then sent him a note on Sunday, asking him to send his report to the Legation or call there on Monday morning at 8.30. "...On Monday morning I was very much surprised still to receive no news from M. Kirschen, and I called at his house at 12.30; but I was informed that he would not be there till about the end of the afternoon. I then called, at 12.40, at the house of another lawyer interested in the case of a fellow-prisoner, and found that he also was out. In the afternoon, however, the latter lawyer called at my house, saying that in the morning he had heard from the German Kommandatur that judgment would be passed only the next morning — viz. Tuesday morning. He said that he feared that the Court would be very severe for all the prisoners.

"Shortly after, this lawyer left me." And that is the last that has been heard of M. Kirschen.

On Sunday evening, the narrative of the trial which we have quoted above was communicated to M. de Leval by a private person who had been a witness of the proceedings; and on receipt of this information, M. de Leval did not wait to hear the last of M. Kirschen before addressing himself directly to the German Governor-General's "Political Department." It will be better to give his account of what followed in his own words:

"After I had found out these facts (viz. Sunday evening), I called at the Political Division of the German Government in Belgium and asked whether, now that the trial had taken place, permission would be granted to me to see Miss Cavell in jail, as surely there was no longer any object in refusing that permission.

"I also asked him that permission be granted to Mr. Gahan, the English clergyman, to see Miss Cavell.

"At the same time we prepared at the Legation, to be ready for every eventuality, a petition for pardon, addressed to the Governor-General in Belgium, and a transmitting note addressed to Baron von der Lancken.

"Monday morning at 11 I called up Mr. Conrad on the telephone from the Legation, asking what the Military Court had decided about Mr. Gahan and myself seeing Miss Cavell. He replied that Mr. Gahan could not see her, but that she could see any of the three Protestant clergymen attached to the prison; and that I could not see her till the judgment was pronounced and signed, but that this would probably only take place in a day or two. I asked the German official to inform the Legation immediately after the passing of said judgment, so that I might see Miss Cavell at once, thinking, of course, that the Legation might, according to your intentions, take immediate steps for Miss Cavell's pardon if the judgment really was a sentence of death."

At 11 o'clock on Monday morning *"Herr Conrad gave positive assurances that the Legation would be fully informed as to developments in this case."*

That is, word for word, the categorical statement of Mr. Gibson, Secretary of the United States Legation at Brussels.

"Despite these assurances (Mr. Gibson continues), we made repeated enquiries in the course of the day, the last one being at 6.20 p.m., Belgian time. Mr. Conrad then stated that sentence had not yet been pronounced, and specifically renewed his previous assurances that he would not fail to inform us as soon as there was any news."

To return to M. de Leval's report. "While I was preparing a note about the case, at 8 p.m." he says, "I was privately and reliably informed that the judgment had been delivered at 5 o'clock in the afternoon, that Miss Cavell had been sentenced to death, and that she would be shot at 2 o'clock the next morning."

The death-sentence had been signed at 5 p.m. An hour and twenty minutes after its signature, Herr Conrad had once more assured the American Legation that nothing had happened and all was well. The Legation had learnt the truth at 8 o'clock, and still no intimation of it had been conveyed to them by the competent German authorities. The German authorities never informed them of the truth, until they were taxed with it by emissaries from the Legation itself.

The German authorities informed the American Legation of only one positive fact — the name of Edith Cavell's first, and already superseded, advocate. And the advocate substituted in M. Braun's place gave them knowledge of only one fact more — the date on which the trial was to begin. All the important facts — the fact that the Court had risen; the narrative of what had taken place before it rose, including the supremely important fact that the death-penalty had been demanded; and the final fact that this sentence had already been pronounced — these were communicated to the American Legation by private informants.

VIII
MONDAY NIGHT – "THE POLITICAL DEPARTMENT"

IT was the eleventh hour, yet the American Legation had no thought of abandoning the struggle. In view of this very eventuality they had drawn up the day before two, "pleas for mercy" (requites en grace), of identical purport, but addressed respectively to Baron von der Lancken, the Chief of the Political Department, and to Baron von Bissing, the Governor-General of the Occupied Territory.

Brussels,
October 11, 1915.

Your Excellency,

I have just heard that Miss Cavell, a British subject, and consequently under the protection of my Legation, was this morning condemned to death by court-martial.

If my informant is correct, the sentence in the present case is more severe than all the others that have been passed in similar cases which have been tried by the same court, and, without going into the reasons for such a drastic sentence, I feel that I have the right to appeal to your Excellency's feelings of humanity and generosity in Miss Cavell's favour, and to ask that the death-penalty passed on Miss Cavell may be commuted and that this unfortunate woman shall not be executed.

Miss Cavell is the head of the Brussels Surgical Institute. She has spent her life in alleviating the sufferings of others, and her school has turned out many nurses who have watched at the bedside of the sick all the world over, in Germany as in Belgium. At the beginning of the war Miss Cavell bestowed her care as freely on the German soldiers as on others. Even in default of all other reasons, her career as a servant of humanity is such as to inspire the greatest sympathy and to call for pardon. If the information in my possession is correct, Miss Cavell, far from shielding herself, has, with commendable straightforwardness, admitted the truth of all the charges against her, and it is the very information which she herself has furnished, and which she alone was in a position to furnish, which has aggravated the severity of the sentence passed on her.

It is then with confidence, and in the hope of its favourable reception, that I have the honour to present to your Excellency my request for pardon on Miss Cavell's behalf.

I avail, &c.,
BRAND WHITLOCK.

The American Minister, Mr. Whitlock, himself was ill and confined to his bed. Yet with his own hand he wrote a note of personal intercession.

> My Dear Baron,
>
> I am too ill to present my request to you in person, but I appeal to the generosity of your heart to support it and save this unfortunate woman from death. Have pity on her!
>
> Yours sincerely,
> BRAND WHITLOCK.

This final appeal, as well as the more formal pleas for mercy that had been previously prepared, was taken charge of by Mr. Gibson, the Secretary of the Legation. We quote what followed, from his official report to Mr. Whitlock.

"In conformity with your instructions, I went (accompanied by M. de Leval) to look for the Spanish Minister, and found him dining at the home of Baron Lambert. I explained the circumstances to his Excellency and asked that (as you were ill and unable to go yourself) he go with us to see Baron von der Lancken and support as strongly as possible the plea, which I was to make in your name, that execution of the death-penalty should be deferred until the Governor could consider your appeal for clemency. The Spanish Minister willingly agreed to accompany us, and we went together to the Politische Abteilung.

"Baron von der Lancken and all the members of his staff were absent for the evening. We sent a messenger to ask that he return at once to see us in regard to a matter of utmost urgency. A little after 10 o'clock he arrived, followed shortly after by Count Harrach and Herr von Falkenhausen, members of his staff. The circumstances of the case were explained to him and your note presented, and he read it aloud in our presence. He expressed disbelief in the report that sentence had actually been passed, and manifested some surprise that we should give credence to any report not emanating from official sources.

"Baron von der Lancken stated that it was quite improbable that sentence had been pronounced, that even if so, it would not be executed within so short a time, and that in any event it would be quite impossible to take any action before morning. It was, of course, pointed out to him that if the facts were as we believed them to be, action would be useless unless taken at once. We urged him to ascertain the facts immediately, and this, after some hesitancy, he agreed to do.

"He telephoned to the presiding judge of the court-martial and returned in a short time to say that the facts were as we had represented them, and that it was intended to carry out the sentence before morning.

"We then presented, as earnestly as possible, your plea for delay. So far as I am able to judge, we neglected to present no phase of the matter which might have had any effect, emphasizing the horror of executing a woman, no matter what her offence, pointing out that the death-sentence had heretofore been imposed only for actual cases of espionage, and that Miss Cavell was not even accused by the German authorities of anything so serious. I further called attention to the failure to comply with Mr. Conrad's promise to inform the Legation of the sentence.

"I urged that inasmuch as the offences charged against Miss Cavell were long since accomplished, and that, as she had been for some weeks in prison, a delay in carrying out the sentence could entail no danger to the German cause. I even went so far as to point out the fearful effect of a summary execution of this sort upon public opinion, both here and abroad.

"The Spanish Minister forcibly supported all our representations and made an earnest plea for clemency.

"Baron von der Lancken stated that the Military Governor was the supreme authority ('Gerichtsherr') in matters of this sort. After some discussion he agreed to call the Military Governor on the telephone, and learn whether he had already ratified the sentence, and whether there was any chance for clemency. He returned in about half an hour, and stated that he had been to confer personally with the Military Governor, who said that he had acted in the case of Miss Cavell only after mature deliberation; that the circumstances in her case were of such a character that he considered the infliction of the death penalty imperative; and that in view of the circumstances of this case he must decline to accept your plea for clemency or any representation in regard to the matter.

"Even after Baron von der Lancken's very positive and definite statement that there was no hope, and that under the circumstances 'even the Emperor himself could not intervene' we continued to appeal to every sentiment to secure delay, and the Spanish Minister even led Baron von der Lancken aside in order to say very forcibly a number of things which he would have felt hesitancy in saying in the presence of the younger officers and of M. de Leval, a Belgian subject.

"His Excellency talked very earnestly with Baron von der Lancken for about a quarter of an hour. During this time M. de Leval and I presented to the younger officers every argument we could think of. I reminded them of our untiring efforts on behalf of German subjects at the outbreak of war and during the siege of Antwerp. I pointed out that, while our services had been rendered gladly and without any thought of future favors, they should certainly entitle you to some consideration for the only request of this sort you had made since the beginning of the war. Unfortunately, our efforts were unavailing. We persevered until it was only too clear that there was no hope of securing any consideration for the case.

"We left the Politische Abteilung shortly after midnight, and I immediately returned to the Legation to report to you.

HUGH GIBSON.

IX
MONDAY NIGHT THE PRISON OF ST.-GILLES

THAT is what happened at the "Political Department" of the German Administration in Brussels on the evening of Monday, October 11th. Meanwhile, a very different interview was taking place in the Military Prison of St.-Gilles, where Mr. Gahan, the British chaplain in the Belgian capital, had been admitted at last to visit Edith Cavell at 10 o'clock, five hours after the sentence had been passed and four hours before it was put into execution.

"On Monday evening, the 11th October" (Mr. Gahan writes), "I was admitted by special passport from the German authorities to the prison of St.-Gilles, where Miss Edith Cavell had been confined for ten weeks. The final sentence had been given early that afternoon.

"To my astonishment and relief I found my friend perfectly calm and resigned. But this could not lessen the tenderness and intensity of feeling on either part during that last interview of almost an hour.

"Her first words to me were upon a matter concerning herself personally, but the solemn asseveration which accompanied them was made expressly in the light of God and eternity. She then added that she wished all her friends to know that she willingly gave her life for her country and said: 'I have no fear nor shrinking; I have seen death so often that it is not strange or fearful to me. . . .'

"She further said: 'I thank God for this ten weeks' quiet before the end. . . .'

"'Life has always been hurried and full of difficulty. . . .'

"'This time of rest has been a great mercy. . . '

"'They have all been very kind to me here. But this I would say, standing as I do in view of God and eternity, I realize that patriotism is not enough. I must have no hatred or bitterness towards anyone.'

"We partook of the Holy Communion together, and she received the Gospel message of consolation with all her heart. At the close of the little service I began to repeat the words 'Abide with me,' and she joined softly in the end.

"We sat quietly talking until it was time for me to go. She gave me parting messages for relations and friends. She spoke of her soul's needs at the moment and she received the assurance of God's Word as only the Christian can do.

"Then I said,' Goodbye,' and she smiled and said, 'We shall meet again.'"

* * * * *

The rest is silence. All we know is the testimony of the German military-chaplain who was with her at the end.

"She was brave and bright to the last. She professed her Christian faith, and that she was glad to die for her country. . . .

"She died like a heroine. . . ."

* * * * *

Beati mortui qui in Domino moriuntur, ut requiescant a laboribus suis; opera enim illorum sequntur illos.

REVELATION, Chapter xiv, 13.

OTHER BOOKS YOU MAY LIKE

Nurse at the Trenches:
Letters Home from a WW1 Nurse
Agnes Warner, ISBN 0951565567

A War Nurse's Diary:
Sketches from a Belgian Field Hospital
Anon, ISBN 0951565575

'Mademoiselle Miss'
Letters from an American Girl in a French Army Hospital at the Front
Anon, ISBN 1905363109

A VAD in France
Olive Dent, ISBN 1905363095

Soldier, Nurse and Spy in the Union Army:
The Adventures and Experiences of a Woman in Hospitals, Camps and Battlefields
Sarah Emma Edmonds, ISBN 184685041X

The Angels of the Battlefields:
The Florence Nightingales of the U.S. Civil War
Brockett & Vaughan, ISBN 1846850428

The Nightingale Sisters,
The Making of a Nurse in 1800's America
Rosalind Franklin, ISBN 0951565583

America's First Trained Nurse
My Life as a Nurse in America, Great Britain and Japan 1872-1911
Linda Richards, ISBN 1846850681

The Nurse's Calling:
Practical Hints to Nurses in the Early 1900's
Harriet Camp Lounsbery, RN, ISBN 0951565591

The Edwardian Baby for Mothers & Nurses
Mrs. J Langston Hewer (Midwife), ISBN 1905363060

When The Nightingale Sang:
A Nurse's Life in the 1950's & 1960's
Rosalind Franklin, ISBN 0951565532

Ambulance No 10:
A Driver's Letters from the French Front
Leslie Buswell, ISBN 1905363036

Only a Dog:
A Dog's Devotion to his Master in the First World War
Bertha Whitridge Smith, ISBN 1905363079

The Padre of Trench Street:
The Priest who gave his life for his men at Ypres
Alfred O'Rahilly, ISBN 190536315X

PLUS MANY MORE!

THESE TITLES CAN BE ORDERED FROM ANY GOOD BOOKSTORE OR BOOK WEBSITE SUCH AS WWW.AMAZON.COM

THEY CAN ALSO BE ORDERED FROM US DIRECT AT **WWW.DIGGORYPRESS.COM**

Printed in the United Kingdom
by Lightning Source UK Ltd.
115572UKS00001B/114

9 781846 852022